THE FUGUE

Volume One

From the Beginnings to Johann Sebastian Bach

BY

ADAM ADRIO

ARNO VOLK VERLAG HANS GERIG KG · KÖLN

No. 19

Table of Contents

Preliminary Note

In the preparation of this volume I have had the extensive support of Dr. Dietrich Manicke and Lars Ulrich Abraham, both of them former members of the Musicological Institute of the Free University in Berlin. I wish to express to them my sincere thanks above all for their help in the selection of the examples herein contained. In view of the immeasurable richness of the historical material, this selection must in all events leave many wishes unfulfilled and will even give rise to certain reservations. The choice of examples designed to illustrate the history of fugal composition in its various stages corresponds to the thesis developed in the Introduction that the fugue is first and foremost an instrumental form and, as such, one conceived particularly in terms of keyboard instruments. Thus the examples begin with compositions in which the divorcement from vocal models has to a large degree already been accomplished. Then the attempt is made to trace chronologically through the examples the process by which the union of Southern conceptions of form with the Northern ideal of polyphony as the form-building element led gradually to the fugue at the fifth, which in the first half of the eighteenth century achieves classical perfection in the fugues of J. S. Bach.

A. A.

Introduction

In Michael Praetorius' "Terpsichore" (1612) the first pages, which form part of the title, contain a piece entitled *Fuga à 3*. The same title is used by Johann Sebastian Bach to designate 3-part fugues in *"Das wohltemperierte Klavier"*; but Praetorius means by this term something entirely different from Bach. Although preceding a work devoted to instrumental dances, his piece is provided with a text:

"Nu, nu, nu,   drei Stim in ein,
nu schall und sih zu,   singt alle nach mir,
wat ein Gsang is dat,   fa di don diri don, don, don,
und wie kann dat sien,   lasst uns frewen und fröhlich sein,
*   la ri don, diri don, don, don."*

This text is vaguely reminiscent of older guessing-canons and more especially of the so-called *Gesellschaftskanon*. The piece is in fact a sung canon, written on one stave. Its only peculiarity consists in the intervals in which the voices enter as indicated by the clefs: the first begins on c, the second on g and the third on d'. This is no reason to assume, however, that at that time "fuga" always meant sung canon, or vice versa that every sung canon was called a "fuga". Hans Leo Hassler called his four-part adaptations of protestant chorales (1607) "Psalms and Christian songs with the melodies set in the manner of a fugue" (German: "fugweis"). "Fugweis" clearly means "fugato" in this context; Hassler used the expression to indicate the strongly imitative style as opposed to the simpler style of the *cantio* pieces, which appeared a year later (composed *simpliciter*).

Hassler's title refers to the peculiarity that in all sections except one (the Benedictus) the superius and tenor move in canon. The imitation is so strict that the second part does not have to be written out; entry signs above the first part are adequate (cf. also Palestrina's "Missa ad Fugam" in "Der Kanon" ed. by Fritz Jöde, Wolfenbüttel, 1926, p. 100 ff.). In Praetorius' Fuga à 3 mentioned above, exactly the same procedure is employed, with regard to the second and third parts.

In his "Istitutioni harmoniche" of 1558 under the heading "Delle Fughe, o Consequence, ouer Reditte, che dire le vogliamo. Cap. 51" Zarlino deals with all manners of canon in usage at his time. He calls the first voice Guida and the imitating voice Consequente, thus employing the Italian names for DUX and COMES (leader and companion).

From the 14th century onwards *fuga* thus means much the same as *caccia*. Their characteristic feature is a technical one – namely, the imitative pairing of voices, generally with the entries comparatively far apart, in a composition of three or more parts. After the appearance of the imitative vocal style, *fuga* also came to mean imitation at the beginning of a piece or section (according to Müller-Blattau first used in this sense by Ramis de Pareja in 1482); then still later the markedly imitative style of a whole piece, as in those works of Hassler that he composed "fugweis" (characteristically, the imitative entry is always at the beginning of a line). Finally *fuga* came to mean *canon* in the strict sense of the word, namely the sung canon, such as Oswald von Wolkenstein's (cf. Fritz Jöde, "Der Kanon", p. 14 ff.). In this case the name indicates a more or less clearly defined smaller musical form, such as the "rotulus", a kind of canon that returns to its point of origin.

That these three meanings of the same term were able to exist side by side unchallenged for so long a time, despite the great differences between them, is due to a common factor that binds them together and connects them as well with the later fugue form of large proportions. This common factor is that of canon.

When we speak of a fugue today, we generally mean the fugue at the fifth. We know that there are other species of fugue, but we tend to regard these as varieties or predecessors of the fugue proper, which was to receive its final form at the hands of Johann Sebastian Bach. To be sure, this point of view hinders the appreciation of the many varieties of this musical form and results in some masterpieces being regarded as mere predecessors. Yet the work of Bach has been chosen as a scale of comparison not arbitrarily but with all the justification of historical fact. However strong the will to objectivity may be, the example set by Bach must be regarded as a norm and as a standard of comparison if the appraisal of the vast amount of material relating to the fugue form is to have any sense at all.

Instead of an abstract definition of the idea "fugue" we prefer the description of a specific composition in order to make clear what is normally meant by this word. Bach provided us with a compendium of fugue-composition in "The Art of Fugue". Whatever conflicting opinions may exist regarding the proper order of the various "Contrapuncti" within the whole work, it is certain that the group of the first four is intended to represent something like the "usual procedure". Thus we may take as an example the third Contrapunctus of the group.

This piece in D minor (No. 11 c) is opened by the tenor, which states the THEME or SUBJECT; it commences on d', falls a fourth, and then rises by way of the notes of the A minor triad to f', its highest point. This part of the theme consists of half notes; two quarter notes of the falling scale bring it back to the half note c' sharp. We have now reached the first half of the fourth bar. The subject is only four bars in length. It is a well known fact that bars 2, 4, 8, 16 and so on play an important part in Lied or song form. They are points at which, for reasons of symmetry, the listener is prepared to accept a concluding figure. The fact that the subject of this fugue is four bars long, might lead one to think that B a c h intended to employ such a concluding figure here. It is important to realize here that this is by no means the case. The length of the subject is of no significance as it is in Lied form, unless it be that the further development of the subject is intended to cover up this potential conclusion. In the case quoted, this is achieved by means of a rhythmical figure: the half note on c′ sharp is tied to an eighth note which, together with the eighth notes a, b and c′ sharp is part of a group of four notes, and which, more especially as the leading tone to d′, leads into bar 5. Whether achieved in this or in any other way, the theme of a fugue must be "open" and capable of further development — not compact, like that of a song.

The alto voice begins with the theme in bar 5. The successive entry of several voices having the same melody is called CANON. The alto begins on a′. Thus we are confronted with a canon at the upper fifth. However it turns out that the melodic intervals do not correspond entirely with those of the tenor; in fact the first interval is not a fourth, but a fifth. This means that the name "canon at the upper fifth" is not really applicable. After the first "false" interval the whole line continues one note too low. It would thus be more appropriate to speak of a canon at the upper fourth with alteration of the first note. This makes the construction of the canon considerably more complicated; in addition, the last bar of the subject in the alto voice contains an important intervallic alteration; instead of the expected f′ sharp f′ natural appears. (The significance of this alteration becomes apparent if one considers that under certain circumstances two comparatively unrelated keys, such as the major and minor based on the same tonic, differ from one another only in a single note, the mediant, without losing any of their independent character as a result.) The consequence of all this alteration is that the tonality established by the tenor is maintained, although the theme appears on a different scale degree. Such a procedure is referred to as a TONAL ANSWER.

As a continuation of the subject, bars 5–8 in the tenor voice are rhythmically more strongly marked and more lively; leaps are avoided, and the melodic line proceeds in small and very small (chromatic) steps, first down to g sharp and then up to f′. As a counterpoint to the alto voice (and thus to the subject) this melodic line forms a clear contrast to, while at the same time growing naturally out of the subject. It is impossible to analyse here in its minute details this very clever combination of melodies; suffice it to say that the contrast of the counterpoint to the subject is advantageous to both voices in that it underlines the peculiar character of the subject while preserving the individual character of the counterpoint; and that it favours the rhythmic factor already mentioned in connection with the conclusion of the subject: the principle of flowing progression.

The two forms of the subject presented by the tenor and alto voices are called DUX and COMES, and in this case the *comes* provides a TONAL answer to the *dux*.

In bar 9 the soprano voice enters with the subject in the *dux* form on d″, without the least alteration. The alto voice now proceeds as the tenor has already done. It continues the subject with the same counterpoint; because of the alteration at the end of the subject, the first note of the counterpoint is a′, and from this note onwards the alto voice imitates the pattern of the tenor in all its intervals. It forms a real canon at the upper fifth, or, in the usual terminology of the fugue, it is a *comes* with a *real* answer. Such a counterpoint is called a COUNTER-SUBJECT.

During bar 9 and the following bars the tenor voice adds to the combination of subject and counter-subject in the treble and alto a free and very marked counterpoint. One of its many peculiarities may be indicated here: we have already observed in the first combination of subject and counter-subject that their complementary rhythms served to carry on the flow of eighth notes begun in the last bar of the subject. Now with its free counterpoint the tenor voice fills out with

its eighth notes the remaining eighth-note gaps, the last one of the entire fugue being on the third beat of bar 9. This fact is of paramount significance and illustrates clearly the principle of flux mentioned above, which pervades every aspect of the fugue.

The influence of this principle is felt in a further detail in bar 13: the entry of the bass, which one expects here, does not occur. After what has gone before it would have produced an effect of absolute symmetry which Bach apparently wished to avoid. For this reason the three-part writing is continued in bars 13 and 14, and the entry of a fourth voice has become problematic for the listener. It may occur either at any moment or not at all. That is the situation when the bass commences with the subject in *comes* form on a in bar 15.

The next four bars (15–18), in which the bass has the subject, follow the given pattern as regards the interplay of subject and countersubject: the part played by the tenor from bar 9 onwards is now taken over by the alto, which forms a free counterpoint to the subject and counter-subject (represented by the bass and the treble) and has the rhythmic function of filling out the gaps in the flow of eighth notes. This also reveals the presence of a plan, which might be designated as the "economy of voices", and which is apparent immediately, as it is in the entire course of the fugue (here, in the first DEVELOPMENT it is especially apparent): each voice states in turn the subject, the countersubject and the free counterpoint. The tenor, which was the opening voice, has already passed through these three stages, and is "exhausted". It makes a temporary pause in bar 16 and then drops out for some time in bar 18. The effect of this economy is of more significance for the whole than it is for the individual parts. A glance at the entire fugue reveals the following: the full texture is continually interrupted — that is to say, it is seldom, and then only for very short periods, composed in four parts. This is not a matter of mere chance. Episodes employing all, or nearly all, voices occur at important stages in the composition and represent a means of dividing the whole into sections — a formal procedure compatible with the stylistic ideal of Bach's fugues, the principle of constant flow. (The reduction of the number of active voices to 2 is also frequently employed as a means of division suitable to the fugue, cf. No. 8 bars 26 ff.) The following scheme may serve to make this principle clear:

Bar 15 ff: interrupted four-part section, approximately 2½ bars:
End of first development
Bar 43 ff: real four-part section, approximately 3 bars:
End of the second development
Bar 51 ff: interrupted four-part section, approximately 5½ bars:
Beginning of the third development
Bar 58 ff: interrupted four-part section, approximately 3 bars:
Climax of the third development
Bar 63 ff: real four-part section, ten bars:
Conclusion of the fugue

Observation of the number of voices employed at any given moment reveals that B a c h plans most carefully in this respect. Extended composition in four active parts is reserved for the conclusion (ten full bars), and in the course of the fugue it occours only briefly at points of climax.

The first DEVELOPMENT ends on the first beat of bar 19. The fact that this conclusion is so easily determined is explained by the very clear construction of the subsequent EPISODE (bar 19 ff). This consists of four ingeniously contrived bars: the treble and alto present an imitation (developed from the COUNTER-SUBJECT) in sequence, which is underlined four times by a short and energetic figure in the bass. Among other things the unusually complicated modulation of this EPISODE is worthy of note. Suffice it to remark here: the composer achieves his aim (to veil the entry of the subject) this time by means of symmetry. However, this symmetry is only one side of the "veiling" process; the other is the alteration of the theme in its following entry. With the entry of the treble in bar 23 (2nd quarter) the second DEVELOPMENT commences. The rhythm of the subject has now been considerably altered and in addition syncopated. It begins on a″ (up to now f″ was the highest note to appear), and as it is based on the form of the c o m e s the note b″flat is reached in the course of this statement. This is the highest note of the whole piece and is heard only once more, namely during the third development (bar 53). The subject is covered by the flow of eighth notes only to appear in a very exposed register. The second development differs from the first in the following points:

1. It is considerably longer (24 as opposed to 18 bars) in spite of the same number of entries.

2. It employs the altered subject three times, and the fourth entry with the original subject occurs only after a fairly long episode.

3. It uses only two voices to state the subject, namely the treble and the tenor, each of which has the theme twice.

4. It does not adhere to the scheme of Dux and Comes.

The greater length stems from the fact that the second and third entries are preceded by two themeless bars (27/28 and 33/34) and the fourth entry is preceded even by four such bars (39–42). Bars 27 and 28 are characterized by a symmetrical structure in the bass; a trill makes this even clearer. At the subsequent entry in bar 29 the subject is still more veiled, being stated by a middle voice. The veiling process continues. It is assisted by bars 33/34, which inconspicuously carry on the material of bar 32. Now the tenor breaks in and quotes the subject in its altered form (bar 35); it has by now approached the limits of recognition. At the previous entry the tenor was at least a newly-added voice, and its first note (e′) was comparatively exposed in the tenor range. The subject now appears in the middle register (beginning on c′) in a voice in which it is least expected and with an arrangement of intervals as yet unfamiliar in the major key. There can be no doubt that this is all part of the highly organized plan; our assumption that the progressive veiling of the subject represented the composer's artistic purpose is borne out. In this respect bars 35 ff represent a sort of apogee; the subject has become almost extinct. To that extent what follows may justly be described as dramatic: the "dead" subject is to be called to life again. For this purpose Bach forms an episode after the pattern of the four bars 19–22, but now reversed – that is to say, in *ascending* sequence. The treble, which for no less than 12½ bars has remained silent, now states, clearly audible above the other parts, the original subject in the form of the *comes*, starting on e″ and accompanied by the countersubject in the alto voice. This brings the second development to a splendid close (bars 43–46). The non-schematic impression given by this work stands in sharp contrast to the strict scheme made apparent by this analysis.

The entries of the subject in the THIRD DEVELOPMENT are arranged as follows: bar 51, bass with the *dux*-form of the original subject on c (but with the conclusion of the *comes*); bar 55, alto (on a′) with the *comes*-form of the altered subject (from the second development), closer to the original subject, however, to the extent that the syncopations have been abandoned; bar 58, treble with the *dux*-form of the same version of the subject on d″; bar 63, tenor with the *comes*-form of the original subject on a. The four-part texture effected by this entry is maintained until the conclusion in bar 72. The counter-subject is used as follows in the third development: it does not accompany the subject in the bass at all; the tenor has it in a slightly altered form on d′ (the head of the subject has been rhythmically and chromatically contracted) as accompaniment to the subject in the alto. The subject in the treble is also heard without it. Finally it appears in the bass, clearly audible in the original form, against the subject in the tenor.

Considering the third development as a whole, one might well ask whether merely counting the citations of the subject is not the easiest way to analyse a fugue into developments and episodes. This is not the case. It is true that in this fugue the distribution of statements of the subject is especially regular: each development section has four statements out of a total of twelve. However that only indicates that this is a fugue of unusual regularity (Bach even does without the stretto here, which he employs so often in other works as a means of increasing tension). In most cases such regularity will not be found.

The 6 final bars, unrelated to the subject, have already been mentioned. It is important to cite one last characteristic: the motion, that is to say the intensity of flow, diminishes to such an extent that in the penultimate bar the voices' activity is reduced to an absolute minimum required to maintain the flow of eighth notes. The pedal point is a typical feature of this reduction in intensity.

The following detailed explanations are designed to show how in the course of time composers developed the technique of short imitations (a long-established technique of vocal polyphony) to a compositional principle capable of producing an independent form.

That the Canzon of Claudio Merulo (No. 1) is derived from vocal polyphony is indicated by the title. The elevation of keyboard instruments (and of the lute) from the rôle of mere accompaniment to full independence was achieved in a roundabout way as the result of their ability to play in several parts and consequently to reproduce complete vocal compositions. Thus we find the names "Misse" and "Mutet" used to designate instrumental versions of masses and motets. In similar manner the chanson occurs as "canzon". Here the chances of developing a musical form appropriate to the instrument and independent of vocal counterpart were much greater. For the chanson, according to Müller-Blattau, "early developed purely musical features: imitation of small basic motifs and independent linear progression of the parts. In the face of this the text became less important, and the chanson could be adapted to instruments without difficulty." Our example, therefore, illustrates a musical genre originating in traditional forms that by assimilating new musical content became the beginning of a whole new development.

Not only the title but even more the piece itself reveals unmistakably its origin in vocal music: as a whole, and especially in the second half ("Abgesang" with repetition), it has a Lied-like character. The only thing that distinguishes it for the listener from a vocal composition played on an instrument are the ornaments. Their importance for the emancipation of instrumental music cannot be overestimated. By means of diminutions an indifferent *res facta* can be transformed into an idiomatic, clearly instrumental work. It is worthy of note that Merulo writes out all the diminutions in full; he does it with a specific purpose, for in the course of the piece most of them gain significance as motifs. A short analysis will show how Merulo solved the central problem of the fugue — namely, how to raise imitation to a principle of composition.

The beginning is clearly that of a fugue. But the connection between this composition and its vocal model explains the use of imitation in pairs, which is opposed to the procedure of the normal fugue. On the other hand this peculiarity of Merulo's Canzon shows its importance as a link in the chain of development. Imitation in pairs was in fact carried over into the classical period of the fugue: the pairing of *dux* and *comes* is a practice which can be observed *in statu nascendi* in this piece by Merulo, notwithstanding its vocal origin.

Closer examination of the piece reveals that in spite of its simple Lied-like character it employs imitation to a remarkable extent and that these imitations have a fugue-like character in that they follow the pattern set at the beginning: in other words, like the beginning they form regular DEVELOPMENTS, ten in number, of which the last three are practically exact repetitions of their three predecessors (Abgesang). Compared with normal fugal practice these developments are not quite regular: they are not all based on the same theme as stated in the opening bars but rather on different themes. Compositions of Italian origin in the 16th century by Marcantonio di Bologna, Cavazzoni, Willaert or Buus for instance, are often characterized by such variety of themes. We may therefore assume that Merulo was not yet familiar with the practice of using one single subject but that he constructed his composition on various motifs with the aid of imitation; these he combined with free passages using independent material.

Exact analysis however reveals a conscious effort towards formal unity of the whole composition. The developments are based on sections, or variations of sections, of one and the same subject. Even the independent passages are more than mere interludes; they have a common origin in the first diminution of the alto voice and its derivations. It was said above that diminutions were an important step towards an instrumental style; they were also an important feature of musical architecture, contributing to the form of the whole work.

In this Canzon Claudio Merulo solved the problem of the fugue as follows: in the exposition the two upper and the two lower voices are distinctly separated, and the two pairs are placed correspondingly close together (stretto). The subject appears in the form of the DUX and in the COMES as tonal answer. The compact effect of the whole is achieved by three means, the first two of which are derived from vocal practice. The first is the general movement of the piece, which is reminiscent of the chanson. The second is the old device of bridging a cadence by commencing a new motif in at least one voice before the cadence is finished. Thirdly, and most important for future developments, is the unity of the thematic material employed. In contrast to that of the classical fugue this unity is not dependent on the integrity of the subject as initially stated. On the contrary, the subject is divided into several motifs, which in turn become the bases of developments. The fact that even the independent passages can be related to the exposition also contributes strongly to the impression of thematic unity. In passages displaying no such unity (for instance bars 36 or 45 ff) the tendency of the art of diminution towards an unmistakably instrumental idiom reaches its apogee. Here the influence of the toccata is felt, which, exploiting the technical and virtuosic possibilities of the instrument, represents the most extreme form of composition not based on vocal models of that time. The influence of certain features of the toccata on this Canzon must be emphasized here.

The Ricercar of Andrea Gabrieli (No. 2) represents a stage of development in which the influence of vocal music has diminished in favor of a more idiomatic instrumental form. We are struck at the very first hearing of this piece by a feature which had to be established through analysis in the case of Merulo — namely, the unity of thematic material. This is the more remarkable since the Ricercar represents the instrumental adaptation of the motet, and the motet is charac-

terized especially by its division into various sections (determined by the text), each of which is based on a different point of imitation. The thematic unity here achieved may be regarded as an emancipation from vocal music, in other words, as a step towards independence in instrumental composition. One element retained from the motet but already stylized in this piece remains a characteristic feature of the ricercar (which existed as an independent form up to the time of the classical fugue, and indeed beyond it as a special form of fugue): the steady rhythm, and the slow, majestic flow of the subject.

Since the thirteen notes of the subject proceed with comparative regularity and contain no clearly-defined motifs, Merulo's practice of dividing the subject into segments cannot be applied here; the division into two halves (with a rest in the middle) is the only solution that offers itself. And the composer does in fact make use of this solution: in bars 23-25, for instance, the treble voice states only the first half, then waits until bar 28 for the repeated statement of the entire subject; in bars 18 ff. the alto states the second half, while the bass is still occupied with its second statement of the subject. This takes place in such a way that the corresponding part of the bass statement is prepared as in a canon — an element of fugal composition which later gains great significance, producing an increase in tension as the result of contraction in the imitation. The second half of the subject is then stated again by the alto (bar 23), while the tenor is occupied with the statement of the complete subject (in the "false" version heard in the bass at the beginning). This process is accompanied by the entry of the treble mentioned above (bar 25), with only the first seven notes; the continuation, two octaves lower, takes place in the proper place in the bass voice. This "wandering subject" procedure continues to be an element of fugal composition in the future; it appears in the same form in other examples of this volume, notably in the Organ Fugue in G minor by J. S. Bach (No. 11a).

As in Merulo's Canzon, the second voice appears in stretto in the opening of Gabrieli's Ricercar. However, this opening is considerably more complicated than Merulo's: it contains six entries, the alto and tenor having two each. Especially worthy of note are the intervals on which the entries take place: tenor, bass, alto, treble, alto and bass on c', f, f', c'', f' and f respectively. The entry tones of 1/2 and 4/5 thus correspond to the classical fugue (with tonal answer). Gabrieli's subject becomes a theme-type for a whole period; one famous later example, among many others, is the first subject of the great Triple Fugue in E flat major by J. S. Bach, in which the entries of the five voices are on b flat, e flat, b' flat, e' flat and B flat. But whereas Bach employs a tonal answer based on e flat, Gabrieli adds a real answer to f in each case, that is to say he writes in canon at the lower fifth, so that this is really a fugue at the fourth, not at the fifth as in the classical form.

The core of the exposition is the repeated stretto canon at the lower fifth between tenor and bass and between alto and treble. How are the two additional entries to be explained?

The fact that both begin on f (or f′) is obviously intended to establish the key, for the tonic is emphasized in this way. The first (additional) entry of the alto may perhaps be explained by the composer's recognition of the fact that c″ in the treble would not yet be texturally appropriate after the tenor and bass; it must be prepared by an entry in the alto range. After that, however the canon-pattern already established by tenor and bass requires still another entry of the alto voice. With the second entry of the bass, the flaw in its first quotation of the subject is made good; at the first statement, the second half of the subject was a fourth too low.

A further way of explaining this complicated opening involves the following considerations. Assuming that the composer regards the canon as a structural unit, the number of voices should be the same as the number of entries. The pair of voices in canon (bars 1–5 and 10–15) would then correspond to the *dux* form of the subject, and the one-voice answer on f (bars 6–10 and 16–20) to the *comes*-form; this first exposition would thus follow the pattern DUX-COMES DUX-COMES. It should now be clear that the development which finally led to the crystallization of the fugue at the fifth was by no means direct and devoid of conflicts.

The striking feature of this opening is also typical for the whole ricercar: the listener has the impression of a certain planned irregularity, which was referred to above in the model fugue by B a c h as intentional veiling. In A. G a b r i - e l i's Ricercar moreover we encounter a number of elements important for the later development of fugal composition. Because of its origin and constructional principles the ricercar cannot achieve the compactness of form observed in No. 1, which stems from the Lied-like character of the piece. For this very reason, and because of the nature of the subject, the composer is forced to devote special attention to compactness and unity. In so doing, he attains a solution of the formal problem, the technical details of which were later modified but never abandoned.

The subject of example No. 3, the Canzone by Giovanni G a - b r i e l i, reveals a completly new feature, which represents an important step towards the instrumentalization of the fugue. This three-bar subject culminates in the third bar in a figure consisting of a fifth plus fourth and filling the compass of an octave. Strangely enough, this figure does not seem to be an appendage; on the contrary it determines the character of the subject. This alone shows how much farther removed from the chanson this Canzone is than the one by Merulo (No. 1).

The opening follows precisely the rules of the classical fugue. Treble, alto, tenor, and bass state the subject successively, never in stretto. The absence of an accompanying voice at the beginning and the successive entry of the voices at intervals equal to the length of the subject itself may be regarded as a further crystallization of the basic structural principle of the fugue. As in the model fugue by Bach, even the hesitation of the fourth entry may be observed; this practice (as was shown in the analysis above) is closely bound up with the very essence of the fugue.

The outward appearance of the piece does not disclose why the composer chose the name Canzone. In the constant employment of one subject, always stated in full, one may observe a similarity with the second rather than with the first of the two examples already described. It is true that the subject is more complex and to that extent more closely allied to M e r u l o's Canzon; but no use is made, as was made by Merulo, of the "analytical" development of the subject. Such an attempt at classification (to be sure, with only two objects of comparison) shows how indistinct the borders are which separate the various kinds of fugues. Only a comparison of their *forms* can establish clearer differences. In the first example the peculiarity described as "Abgesang with repetition" has obviously become a decisive feature of the Canzon. But whereas the vocal origin of Merulo's piece was entirely clear, we find in G a b r i e l i's a highly differentiated kind of stylisation, which is expressed in the following structure: in the second half of bar 48 the point is reached which later corresponds to the conclusion. The only variation in the conclusion is the note G instead of g in the bass and the d″ in the treble, which now replaces the rest. In contrast to the Canzon by M e r u l o, repetition is not begun at once, but the g of the bass, which closes the cadence, becomes the first note in a new development. In the middle of this development the composer reverts to a figure previously used: the fourth beat (in half notes) of bar 56 is identical with the second beat of bar 31. From there onwards the notes (but not the bar-lines) are identical except for the conclusion, which was already mentioned.

To define the Canzone as a fugue based on the chanson form, using examples 1 and 3 to support this theory, would lead at once to a possible misunderstanding. The structure of the two pieces is the same in that in both the second half consists of two parts, the second of which is a repetition of the first. M e r u l o proceeds to the repetition at once (it is separated only by a very striking chord of the secondary dominant) and then changes the diminutions considerably. Giovanni G a - b r i e l i finds a comparatively more elegant solution by introducing the repetition unobtrusively in a completely new section and then continuing identically, as before, as if "dal segno al fine". But it would be erroneous to think that from this time onwards "Canzone" always meant a fugue of this kind. On the contrary, it many not even mean "fugue" at all but may also designate a musical form that leads to the overture or concerto grosso by way of the orchestral sonata. It can only be said of the canzone as a fugal form that its formal structure relates it to the chanson. As the latter is in itself not a clearly defined genre, but includes a large number of variants (as does the German Lied), its influence may be recognized in various Lied-like features. At this point examples 6 and 8 may be mentioned, in which such Lied-like features are evident, as they are in the later Canzona in D minor (BWV 588) by B a c h.

The formal elements taken over from the chanson by the canzona are of less importance for the development of the fugue than those compositional practices which determined its structure. In Giovanni Gabrieli's Canzone the form of the chanson is stylized to such an extent that, paradoxically enough, he can dispense with the advantages obtainable by making the form as strict as possible. The central problem of the fugue, to create a form with the stylistic means of imitation, has here been so brilliantly solved that the composer seems to amuse himself by juggling the Lied element. The fact that Bach wrote no other canzona than the one mentioned would also seem to indicate that this element is not essential to the fugue.

Perfection of fugal composition is revealed in the following details of example 3: the expressly instrumental character of the subject already mentioned, and the exceptionally clear disposition of the opening. A detailed discussion of the questions arising from the tonal answer cannot be undertaken here any more than in the analysis of the model fugue. Suffice it to say that the manner established by G. Gabrieli becomes the rule as in the minor key the subdominant tendency of the *comes* becomes increasingly strong with the growing stabilization of major-minor harmony. A third peculiarity represents an important enrichment of fugal technique and also originates outside the sphere of polyphonic composition: the varying harmonization of the subject. As a form of polyphonic music the fugue grew up in an age characterized by the consolidation of functional harmony; indeed, it achieved its climax at the same time as the latter (Bach). This fact must be expressly emphasized, lest the other stages of development should be wrongly appraised. It is only natural that Gabrieli is restricted in his use of keys: the subject occurs only on the degrees given by *dux* and *comes* and is not transposed. A comparison of bars 21/22 and 29/30 shows what fine differentiation Gabrieli is capable of in this respect. It cannot be overlooked that all the latent possibilities that later generations will exploit are already opened up here within the limits of the restricted use of keys.

The consideration of Jan Pieterszon Sweelinck's "Fantasia" (No. 4) must be prefaced by some remarks about this term. It is mentioned by Praetorius in "Syntagma musicum III" together with the capriccio and applied to pieces of an improvisatory nature. It is interesting that even as regards terminology a tendency becomes apparent which has often been signalled above as an essential feature of the fugue: the fiction of "unplanned" composition, which is maintained by all kinds of devices, even in pieces of the greatest perfection. This principle is also expressed in the etymology of the word "ricercar".

Confronted with the enormous length of this work, we may well ask how the formal problem is to be solved here through means with which we are already acquainted. We might assume that only the development of *several* subjects could be of avail. But we soon learn that the whole piece is based on a single subject. Furthermore, this subject appears almost without exception on the degrees established in the exposition, so that harmonic modifications, which could be useful in contrasting lengthy sections, do not occur. And yet very few of the 317 bars are independent of the subject. This means that the composer needs a completely different principle of composition which will enable him to achieve contrast in spite of the limitations already mentioned.

The means used by Sweelinck are astonishingly simple and novel:

1. The subject appears, after all the means mentioned have been exhausted, in an altered form: the length of the notes is doubled, quadrupled and finally halved. Towards the end the original form re-appears.
2. The expositions with the augmented subject are so constructed that for the length of each statement characteristic (and almost independent) short movements are created, in which the contrapuntal voices maintain and develop a striking motif.

This technique is easy to follow in the printed music. It is only necessary to add a few remarks about its origin and about two further peculiarities of this composition.

It need not be stressed that the art of augmentation was nothing new; suffice it to mention the practices of the earlier Netherlands School. The instrumental solution of the problems arising from the resulting relationship of the note values had also long since been achieved. For this an abundance of proofs is offered by organ-masses and *cantus firmus* compositions of the early 16th century, in which the c. f. appears in augmentation, hardly recognizable as a melodic line (the *breve* and the *longa* are often employed), while the other voices have striking figures and passages consisting of shorter and even very short notes. If one accepts the thesis that Sweelinck's subject is treated here as a cantus firmus, a historical explanation of his technique offers no difficulty. The novelty consists in the playful treatment of the various episodes. In this respect Sweelinck brought to the development of the fugue as an instrumental form elements of a long-standing, autonomous instrumental tradition: the art of the virginalists.

Also worthy of note are the tonal disposition (Dorian mode) of the piece — especially in the real answer of the *comes;* and an important new feature of fugal composition growing out of the enormously increased importance of the subject: the counter-subject. It is introduced by the alto and the bass in the development in bars 59–84 and provides the thematic material for *fugato* passages in bars 85–122.

Although Samuel Scheidt, a pupil of Sweelinck, called the composition quoted here as example no. 5 "Fuga", he probably intended no conscious distinction from the form coined by Sweelinck. In actual fact the two pieces are astonishingly similar. It may therefore suffice to point out the most important differences.

Although it has the same breadth, the same rhythmical character of the subject, and the same order of entries, the opening presents quite a different picture. It has five entires: treble, alto, tenor, bass and again treble. This additional entry of the treble must be regarded as a means of establishing the key. This is necessary, since the answer is heard at the lower fifth, although the piece is in the major key (see above). We have already pointed out the importance of the development of the answer at the fifth (upper fifth or lower fourth) as it affects tonality. It must now be added that the typical scheme of the fugue at the fifth corresponds to the relation tonic — dominant — in other words, that the *dux-comes* canon at the fourth and at the fifth differ from each other in the significance attached to the initial voice: in the latter it is subordinate, whereas in the former it is the leading voice. The bearing of this fact on the stability of key feeling in the entire piece is apparent. In Samuel Scheidt's Fuga the stability of the tonic is re-established by means of the additional entry of the *dux*.

The second important difference lies in the constant flowing movement. Scheidt succeeds in adapting Sweelinck's fruitful ideas in such a way that they are assimilated in what we might call today, in retrospect, a typically fugal idiom. An outward manifestation of this is the abandonment of Sweelinck's strict division into sections in favor of a more complete formal fusion. Sometimes it is hard to distinguish the development from the other sections. We must not overlook the fact that such differences may be expressions of local idioms; fugues by southern composers tend towards a division into sections. Finally two lesser differences should be cited, which, like those mentioned above, constitute a further development of certain elements observed in Sweelinck's piece. One of them has to do with the growing instrumentalization of the material, which in Scheidt's work has become a more integral part of the substance. This is illustrated by the progression in thirds c′ a f d in the tenor and c A F D in the bass (bar 107) and by other passages as well. The other difference is concerned with the integrity of the subject. In Sweelinck's work we noted that the theme was treated like a cantus firmus — that is to say, it was expanded or contracted in larger or smaller note values without loss of its typical pattern. Scheidt combines both processes — an important indication of the attitude of composers towards the subject. For despite the free treatment of rhythm, the subject as such is given great prominence as a predominantly *melodic* element — a fact which is of prime importance for the future. Sweelinck's inclusion of variation technique in his polyphonic works was based on a rigid treatment of the subject to such an extent that the subject became the structural frame for practically homophonic sections. Seen in this light, Scheidt restored its linear quality — a fact which is expressed clearly in the notation: Scheidt writes in score and in so doing respects clearly the individuality of the voices. In contrast Girolamo Frescobaldi published his Canzona (No. 6) in organ tablature (see facsimile). It is true that the outward appearance of Italian tablature resembles that of normal music; but, ignoring the melodic continuity as it does, it is nevertheless a diagrammatic representation in the true sense of the word. Its transcription into our system of staves gives rise to many difficulties, not the least of which is the proper placement of rests, so important in polyphonic music (see notes).

The very first page of the facsimile reveals elements of Lied-form: at the end of the third line is found a repeat-sign affecting two pages. In this case what was merely suggested above has been put into practice. Symmetry, the basis of Lied-form, is here expressed in its purest form, namely in exact repetition. However, Lied-form need not always be simple. In this case a highly differentiated form has come

into being under the express influence of Lied elements, combined with an astonishingly rich development of imitation and the almost uninterrupted citation of the subject.

This composition contains all those elements which we observed in the first five examples; many however are found here in a more advanced stage of development. But one important element, more or less clearly defined in the previous examples, is lacking: the tendency towards smooth, even flow. On the contrary, the piece is clearly divided into sections — a characteristic that stems to some extent from the local differences mentioned above. On the other hand — and it is hard to decide which of the two elements is cause and which effect — this kind of fugal technique is unimaginable *without* a clear divsion into sections. Strictly speaking, moreover, the ideal of flux has not really been abandoned in this work; it has only been restricted to the shorter single sections and thus does not affect the form as a whole.

The striking novelty of this piece is without doubt its harmony. The subject, which descends chromatically, practically demands the harmonization tonic-secondary dominant-dominant seventh-tonic. And indeed in most cases, especially in the *comes*-form (e. g. bars 23–25), the subject is supported by this harmonic progression. When we recall the surprising effect of the double dominant chord in Merulo's piece (No. 1, bar 36), the vast difference in style separating these two pieces becomes apparent.

This peculiarity must be considered before examining the treatment of the subject in the exposition. The mere observation, based on the printed text, that the answer is at the lower fifth does not tell the whole story; in this piece the *comes* presents that form of answer, later so frequent, which cannot be classified under the headings tonal and real. The nature of the subject is such that it produces a tonal answer disguised as a real answer. The contradiction may be explained by the composer's use of a certain harmonic ambiguity. A very simple example will make clear what is meant. One possibility of analysing the notes d—e in a melody is to consider the d as a suspension before e. In this case the harmonization of this pair of notes will be based on e. On the other hand e can be considered as a passing-note between d and f or f sharp; the accompanying chord will then be based on d. Example 6 is much more complicated, as the harmonic ambiguity is aided by the chromatic nature of the subject. But in principle it is the same situation as in the simplified example just quoted. The consequence is that in spite of the real answer the outside notes of the *dux* form a fifth (d″—g′), whereas those of the *comes* form a fourth (g′—d′). Harmony has thus for the first time become a decisive element in the fugue.

The subject contains another feature highly significant for the future. The process of instrumentalization has already been mentioned and defined as first of all the emancipation of instrumental music from the vocal idiom and then as the tendency towards truly idiomatic writing for (keyboard) instruments. A further development may now be observed; the musical substance — indeed, its very core, the subject — has been created not only for a keyboard instrument but for a *specific* keyboard instrument – namely, the organ. This is most apparent in a certain kind of figure which we may call pedal-progression and which is based on the alternation of left and right feet – an easy figure to execute even at a rapid tempo. In the subject the pedal-progression is to be found in the second bar (a group of four sixteenth notes on the third beat). That idiomatic writing for the pedals can also produce a more highly differentiated kind of figure is shown in the bass part of bar 7. Such figures may also be regarded as criteria for an idiomatic organ style.

It has already been mentioned that the Lied influenced the fugue form as a whole in a very complex manner. Pursuing this influence further, we discover an astonishing fact. Obviously the Lied is something quite foreign to the fugue. The canzone, apparently, took on a typically fugal character only to the extent that it cast aside more and more of its Lied-like elements derived from the chanson and at the same time incorporated such aspects of the chanson as were compatible with the new form. Astonishingly enough, Frescobaldi solves the real problem of fugue with the help of Lied form. The variation form, derived directly from the strophic Lied, is here carried over into the fugue in that the subject – in a new arrangement and new rhythm – supplies the material for a new miniature fugue which, when viewed in its broad context, takes on the character of a development – in other words, of an integrated part of the whole. To avoid the danger inherent in an endless series of such developments, Frescobaldi makes use of another device of Lied composition; in the last section he repeats the subject in its original form (bars 70 ff), but avoids a mere repetition of the opening. The whole has a most natural effect and represents an exemplary compactness of formal structure.

Johann Jakob Froberger, the South German master of piano suites and a pupil of Frescobaldi, calls his fugue Capriccio (No. 7). A comparison of this facsimile with the piece by Frescobaldi however reveals a fact indicating Froberger's independence rather than dependence: Froberger writes in score. As regards form, however, he clearly follows the example of his master although not without reshaping it in his own way by simplifying the form into a clear three-part structure.

In these two peculiarities – the linear concept and the clear, Lied-like division of the whole – we may recognize Froberger's historical position between North and South. Suffice it to indicate the tripartite form based on Frescobaldi's technique; the printed page tells the rest. Worthy of note is the clear and almost pedantically exact form of the "miniature fugues" (sections). The G minor of this piece is colored by the Dorian mode and leads (more than the later G minor) into the regions of F major and D minor.

This piece, in no sense comparable in stature to Frescobaldi's, represents a South German-Austrian version of the fugue, which continued to preserve its identity alongside the northern and southern types. Froberger's Capriccio is similar in nature to the suite; to that extent the question of terminology is not without importance. The term fugue, which originally meant much the same as "development" in

the sense we have here adopted, was applied by Scheidt (No. 5) to the composition as a whole; this is presumably an unconscious indication of what the composer regarded as the most important constructive principle of the form. It is equally illuminating that Froberger chose the less formal title Capriccio for his work – to indicate a looser, freer construction.

The next example, the Fuga by Johann Pachelbel (No. 8), brings us back to the region of the fugue proper. But this piece is also no classical or regular fugue. Its subject is one of those which later become prototypes and is unusually idiomatic for the pedal. Even the kind of counter-subject here used (bars 6/7, alto or 11/12, treble) represents a pattern which will constantly re-appear; the most prominent example is the Fugue in D major by Bach (BWV 532).

Pachelbel's fugue is in binary form. Its structure is clear, though the flow is uninterrupted. The division is achieved in the episode (bars 26 ff.) by means of shorter notes and two-part writing (treble and alto). Up to this episode the flow has been maintained so constantly that the whole section must be regarded as the exposition; it contains five statements of the subject by only three voices. The five entries resemble the entries of a five-voice fugue, not only in the succession of *dux* and *comes*, but also in their arrangement, so that the critical entry of the fourth voice produces true four-part polyphony for three beats (bar 17). The fifth entry (bar 22) is heard clearly as an additional voice by virtue of its exposed position. This short four-part passage in bar 17 is symptomatic, as the rest of the piece reveals; the occasional rejection of the normal relationship of voices is due to southern influences.

Pachelbel's solution of the central problem of the fugue is an extreme one, for his economical use of the thematic material can hardly be surpassed: not only the subject and counter-subject are maintained, but also a counter-subject pair. The following calculation may show to which consequences this leads. The piece has 61 bars. The subject consists of four bars (as opposed to the shorter subjects of the two preceding examples) and is stated eleven times. That means that during 44 bars the whole combination of voices is predetermined, for if the subject and the counter-subject pair sound together as three voices, no place remains for an additional free voice. This rigid scheme is relieved to a certain extent, however, for in each instance the countersubject pair accompanies the subject for only 2½ bars; the first two statements of the subject must of course be excluded from the calculation; and one statement of the subject, the fifth of the exposition (bars 22 ff), appears without the counter-subject pair. Yet this schematic layout is astonishing enough, leading as it does to mere repetition or re-arrangement of the constant combination of voices (e. g. bars 31 and 51 ff).

All this is one aspect of the struggle to create a form which has been justified by the subsequent course of musical history. It is largely in the contradiction between apparently purposeless freedom of form and the strictest principles of construction that the aesthetic appeal of the fugue has its origin.

The particular form of the fugue practiced in Southern Germany and Austria has hitherto been illustrated only by Froberger's Capriccio (No. 7). The Fugues (Nos. 9a and 9b) by Johann Caspar Ferdinand F i s c h e r may be regarded as later examples of this particular form. F i s c h e r was contemporary with B a c h , and these fugues reflect the change of style which had taken place in the meantime. Only their brevity distinguishes them from the norm. The first has two expositions, while the others have only one each. This form of composition may seem strange at first, yet it is a logical consequence of the forms of fugal technique developed in the south: F i s c h e r faces the fact that the fugue as a major form is beyond his reach. In doing so he restores the term "fugue", strictly speaking, to its original, or at least to its earlier, meaning of "development".

The six fugues do not stand alone in F i s c h e r 's "Blumenstrauss", but are enclosed by a prelude and postlude. The question thus arises whether it is not perhaps wrong to regard these miniature fugues as forms in themselves whereas the composer himself may have considered them only within the framework of the whole. Some parallels in these pieces reminiscent of variation form would seem to support this point of view. And yet the thesis is not valid. It is of little importance whether the fugues were to be played singly and were intended, by their brevity, to fit into catholic forms of worship (M ü l l e r - B l a t t a u), or whether they were intended for cyclical performance. In the music itself they appear unequivocally as single pieces. F i s c h e r 's miniature fugues clearly mark the end of the independent South German fugue.

In another sense as well the question which has just been raised is of significance beyond the particular case. Hitherto we have not mentioned the possibility that the fugue, as a form in its own right, might also be subject to limitations. In many cases, however, not only in that of J. C. F. F i s c h e r , the fugue appears in connection with other pieces; the classical pair, Prelude and Fugue (e. g. Nos. 10 and 11 a) is only one of many. An investigation should be made of the relative importance of the component parts in such combinations, and of those artistic considerations which made such a framework for a fugue desirable in some cases and superfluous in others. But such questions cannot be answered in the relatively small compass of this work. Suffice is to point out that our conception of the fugue as a compact work in itself is by no means rendered invalid by such objections. Fugue-like episodes from larger works (church sonatas, French overtures, toccatas, suites) are obviously not dealt with here; the same demands of formal stability cannot be made of them when they are integrated into the larger work. Furthermore we are justified in regarding the fugue as a work in itself because of the notation (concluding double bar) and because of its separate designation (e. g. Prelude and Fugue, that is to say, a combination of two individual forms).

What we have described as instrumentalization reaches its climax in Dietrich B u x t e h u d e 's fugue (No. 10). He achieves a synthesis of fugal writing and virtuosity as it is found in the toccata in such a way that both are naturally combined. In view of the work's length, his methods of achieving this balance are hard to recognize, but the effect is entirely convincing.

B u x t e h u d e , whom Albert S c h w e i t z e r rightly calls "the greatest organist between S c h e i d t and B a c h ", reveals himself as a master through the universality and freedom of imagination in his work, which is neither pedantic nor bound by local tradition. Like his successor B a c h , he must have been able to assimilate every influence and to make use of what was essential in it. Only in this way can we explain his ability to combine the most various practices of composition into an organic whole – and this despite the fact that he spent his entire life in a relatively restricted geographical area.

It is not surprising that we cannot fit this fugue into one of the usual categories; even the designation "Tokkatenfuge" proposed by M ü l l e r - B l a t t a u is too restricted in its meaning.

The tripartite construction of B u x t e h u d e 's piece has the same relationship to that of the canzone as the rondo has to the series of variations; it is a tripartite form of a higher order, further removed from the strophic principle of the Lied. Its novelty consists in the fact that those sections constructed as fugues repeatedly create a tight polyphonic texture after sections of free, imaginative figuration and chordal passages (M ü l l e r - B l a t t a u). In this way B u x t e h u d e succeeds in establishing a vast musical form (138 bars), which combines the advantages of clear structure and uninterrupted flow; the single parts are not merely a mechanical series but the product of energy generated by opposing principles of composition. Herein lies B u x t e h u d e 's greatest contribution to the development of the fugue.

Certain details of his manner of dealing with the subject are also worthy of note. In the first section the *comes* form is prevalent in all developments following the exposition (of 14 entries only one is in the *dux* form); the subject of the third section in strongly reminiscent of that of the first; in the second part the subject is also used *in motu contrario* (bars 50 and 55 ff); the unity of the thematic material is increased in the first fugue by the fact that the counterpoint is derived from the subject, partly through rhythmic analogy; the range of the notes on which the entries occur is extraordinarily large (from d to d sharp). B u x t e h u d e 's fugal form was in its very nature not suitable for imitation. One of the few compositions in which features of this fugue may be recognized is the Triple Fugue in E flat major by B a c h , which represents both a development and a fulfillment of the form.

It was explained at the beginning of this essay why the Contrapunctus from "The Art of Fugue" (No. 11 c) may be regarded as a representative example. Nothing need be added here to the analysis of the piece. In the Organ Fugue (No. 11 a) the influence of P a c h e l b e l is unmistakably clear. The following short analysis will show to what extent other influences are distinguishable.

The subject, which has five (!) bars, is clearly divided into three parts, of which the second (bars 3/4) is eminently idiomatic for the pedals. The treble commences on g'. While the alto begins the *real* answer on d' in bar 6, the treble has the counter-subject. After one and a half bars of development (bars 11/12) the tenor commences with the *dux* on g in bar 12, during which the treble motion ceases. In bar 17 the bass (pedal) begins to state the real *comes*, and the conclusion of the subject is altered to avoid the sixteenth note run. From bar 22 onwards the treble and alto have an interlude, a mock imitation, independent of the subject, while the tenor maintains the flow of sixteenth notes. The tenor commences the second development on g in bar 25, but passes the subject on to the treble after an intermediate bar and continues with the counter-subject. In bar 33 the alto begins on b flat, also to pass on the subject to the tenor after two bars (crossing of voices). There is a short development until the bass enters on B flat in bar 41 omitting, as in the opening, the runs at the end of the subject. The episode from bar 45 onwards corresponds to the first, except that it is in four voices. The third and last development begins in bar 50 with the treble on c″. The sixteenth notes of the counter-subject now appear as a third voice in the pedal. After that the next entry of the subject might be expected, but instead the already familiar episode appears again and leads into a mighty harmonic and figurational climax. In bar 63 the bass enters with the subject on g, once more altering its conclusion for the cadence. The final chord (bar 68) is G major.

The subordination of polyphony to harmony and figuration is remarkable. The counter-subject has the character of an accompanying figure, which provides the subject with harmonic fullness without the need of a further voice. The number of entries of the subject decreases in the course of the piece, and the texture becomes thinner instead of thicker. Everything is designed to make the subject clearly audible, and its entry is such an "event" that it practically takes the place of a whole exposition, as in bars 50 ff. The influence of "Italian models" suggested by H. Keller may well be responsible for such practices. As opposed to other compositions in the Italian manner (e. g. the Canzona in D minor, which is consciously archaic in style) this is an eminently modern piece, dispensing as it does with strict voice leading in favour of sheer sound and centering attention on the main voice.

The same cannot be maintained of the Piano Fugue (No. 11b). In this piece the influence of Pachelbel is apparent in many details, the most obvious of which is the presence of a counter-subject pair (see above) in the three-part sections (bars 9 ff). Bach goes even further however in his restriction of the musical material to that stated in the exposition; indeed the subject itself contains inner relationships, as the sixteenth note group of its first half appears inverted in the second half. A further parallel: the exposition has four entries (up to bar 16); just as in Pachelbel's fugue the additional entry gives the impression of an actual further voice.

This brings us back to the point at which this essay began, for the analysis of the last fugue (No. 11c) has already been made. These three examples give a good idea of how the various lines of development converge in the work of Bach. This fact can only be proved completely by an intensive study of Bach's work. The organ fugues and those of "Das wohltemperierte Klavier" provide a complete picture of the possibilities implied by the term "instrumentalization" in this essay; in Bach's work fugal composition and the exigencies of instrumental technique have found their complete fusion. "The Musical Offering" and "The Art of Fugue" on the other hand provide a "purer" embodiment of the fugal ideal. The emancipation of composition from the bonds of performability (at the keyboards) enables Bach to employ unhindered all those imitative practices which were encountered in rudimentary form in the examples here discussed in connection with the central problem of the fugue — namely, the raising of imitation to the main constructive principle. Bach solved this problem in a manner not to be excelled; the principle of canon predominates in all its forms, from the simplest (canon at the unison) by way of more complicated ones (canon at various intervals and in stretto) to the most highly differentiated (augmentation and diminution); the crowning glory is such large-scale imitation as involves entire groups of voices, as represented by fugues in contrary and retrograde motion or double, triple and quadruple fugues. In Bach's work the fugue has become a real element of composition and thus of musical substance in the true sense of the word. The art of imitation, ever present in Bach's compositions (in the arias and choral pieces, in the choral preludes, in the inventions, suites and orchestral compositions), is not to be compared with that which formerly served as a basis for the development of fugue-like forms. Bach's imitation is derived directly from the fugue and openly follows fugal patterns. From now on imitation is always *fugato*, that is to say, imitation in the manner of a fugue.

The examples presented here are intended to illustrate the progressive development of imitation as a constructive principle and to reveal the fugue as the result of this process. After this consolidation had been achieved, the process continued in a quite different and opposite direction: the fugato was raised to the norm as a technique of composition. This will be illustrated by the examples of Volume II.

To No. 6

First page of Girolamo *Frescobaldi*'s Canzona Terza from the Secondo
Libro di Toccate, Canzone etc., Rome 1627, N. Borboni (Copy of the
Austrian National Library, Vienna)

To No. 7

Opening and closing sections from Johann Jakob *Froberger*'s Capriccio, Autograph of the Austrian National Library, Vienna

Canzon

Claudio Merulo (1533 - 1604)

Ricercar

2

Andrea Gabrieli (1510-1586)

3 # Canzone

Giovanni Gabrieli (1557-1612)

Fantasia

Jan Pieterszon Sweelinck (1562 - 1621)

Fuga

Samuel Scheidt (1587 - 1654)

6 Canzona

Girolamo Frescobaldi (1583-1643)

7 Capriccio

Johann Jakob Froberger (1616-1667)

Fuga

8

Johann Pachelbel (1653-1706)

9a

Fuga

Johann Caspar Ferdinand Fischer (ca.1650‑1746)

9b

Sechs Fugen

Johann Caspar Ferdinand Fischer (ca. 1650 - 1746)

Fuga I

Fuga II

56

Fuga III

Fuga IV

Fuga V

Fuga VI

10 Fuga

Dietrich Buxtehude (1637 - 1707)

11a

Fuga

Johann Sebastian Bach (1685 - 1750)

11b   # Fuga

Johann Sebastian Bach (1685 - 1750)

11c

Contrapunctus

Johann Sebastian Bach (1685-1750)